Kokopelli

Casanova of the Cliff Dwellers

John V. Young

D1475492

Filter Press, LLC
Palmer Lake, Colorado

Published by Filter Press, LLC
P.O. Box 95 • Palmer Lake, CO 80133
888-570-2663
FilterPressBooks.com
Printed in the United States of America on acid free paper.

Illustrations

Photographs are by John V. Young and Gilbert L. Campbell.

Drawings and sketches from other sources cited in the text are by Heather Hamilton.

Drawings on pp. 5 and 14 are by Gail E. Haley from *Kokopelli: Drum in Belly* (Filter Press, 2003).

Other illustrations are from early travel and scientific books and publications of the late 19th century.

Gila Bend Kokopelli in southwestern Arizona. Compare with Chaco and Oraibi figures. Drawing by Heather Hamilton after Waters.

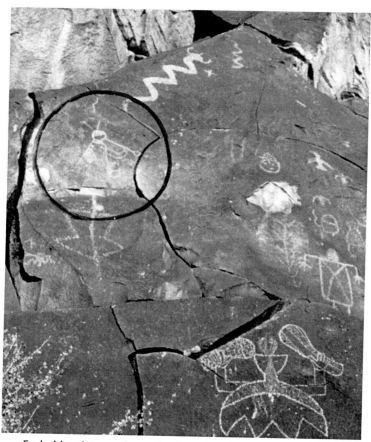

Faded by time and weathering, the Flute Player is among
petroglyphs in the Rio Grande Canyon between Los Alamos
and Santa Fe. Note the recent addition of a plumed serpent.
Photograph by John V. Young.

Publisher's Note

Kokopelli, the traveling salesman, may have used the flute as a notice to villagers that he was coming in peace and was not an enemy sneaking up on them.

Certainly, he has modern counterparts. In Belize, Central America, a group of peddlers take back trails into the remote towns and villages, riding bicycles.

They are known as *Cobaneros*, since many start from the Guatemalan city of Coban. Their predecessors carried shell and tropical goods to the northern pueblos, trading for turquoise. The Cobaneros bring small consumer goods, some textiles, and trade for money. Today they are considered smugglers. Earlier they were not, as there were no national boundaries.

Images and likenesses of Kokopelli, from whimsical to exact reproductions of the ancient rock art, are at tourist stops and gift shops all over the Southwest. Wrought iron and steel cutouts adorn lawns. Kokopelli jewelry from earrings to toe rings is popular. Books about Kokopelli abound. Kokopelli figures decorate walls, trail markers, countless coffee/tea mugs, and are the subject of sculptures in plastics and marble.

Kokopelli in Chaco Canyon in New Mexico. Drawing by Heather Hamilton after Waters.

Kokopelli's Trail is a 142-mile mountain bike trail from Loma in western Colorado to Moab, Utah. Built as a joint effort of the Colorado Plateau Mountain Bike Trail Association (COPMOBA), the Bureau of Land Management, and the U.S. Forest Service, it was blessed by a delegation of Hopi Indians from Arizona. The trail markers show Kokopelli, with a bicycle and mountains in the background.

One wonders what the Ancient Ones would have thought of all this. Their images were chiseled in stone with stone tools. Kokopelli, the deity, was a benign minor god, that brought abundant rain and food to the People.

Interest in Kokopelli has grown since this book was published in 1990. Gilbert Campbell, then publisher of Filter Press, and John V. Young, his friend and fellow historian, put together a general summary of the significance of the figure and where to find Kokopelli pictographs and petroglyphs.

The book has satisfied the curiosity of thousands of visitors to the Southwest. We hope you enjoy and learn from it.

Hunchbacked Flute Player in cave on Pajarito Plateau, west of Santa Fe. The spear point may be a later addition by vandals. Photograph by John V. Young.

*The Flute Player in Oraibi on the Hopi Third Mesa
is much like those at Gila Bend and Chaco.
Drawing by Heather Hamilton after Waters.*

El Morro, now Inscription Rock National Monument, near Gallup, New Mexico. Thayer, Marvels of the New West, 1893.

Introduction

Everywhere that primitive Man roamed the American Southwest, as well as in many other places in the world, he left an enduring record of his passing fancies and urgencies in the form of pictures on rocks.

Those painted on rock surfaces are called *pictographs*. Those incised in the rock surface by pecking or scratching with a stone tool are called *petroglyphs*. To us, many of the designs are undecipherable, but many others seem to be more or less obvious representations of the antelope, bighorn sheep, bears, wolves, coyotes, buffalo, turkeys, cranes, serpents, frogs, lizards and insects.

Hands and feet often appear, sometimes with six digits. Figures of men are depicted fighting, hunting, or apparently doing nothing at all. Other designs almost certainly represent the sun, moon, stars, lightning, clouds, rain and corn — always corn, that sacred and indispensable New World gain originally known as maize. Some signs tell of water springs, trails, or the abode of spirits.

Others could be rebus writing: the representation of words by pictures of objects whose names sound (in the aboriginal language) like the intended words, as in our parlor game of charades.

Why did the ancient people go to all that trouble? As a guess, some of the symbols were intended to invoke good or to repel evil, to assure a crop or to assist in childbirth. But probably nobody will ever know for certain what all of the Southwest's millions of pictographs and petroglyphs were supposed to mean or to do, since they never attained the status of a written language.

Many of the figures might well have been nothing more than the product of idle doodling by people with time on their hands and a smooth surface to scribble on. People still do it, but now usually it is called graffiti.

Newspaper Rock State Park, Utah displays hundreds of petroglyphs under cliff overhang. Photograph by John V. Young.

Casanova of the Ancient Ones
The Hunchbacked Flute Player

Of the multitude of miscellaneous drawings, paintings and scratchings on the rocks and in the caves of the pre-Columbian people of the Southwest, only one anthropomorphic subject can claim both an identity and a proper name as well as gender. Without question, that figure is decidedly male.

Kokopelli's frequent and widespread appearance on pottery and in pictography suggest that he was a well-traveled and universally recognized deity of considerable potency.

A personality, an individual, the personification of a legend, a beneficent god to some and a confounded nuisance

Kokopelli, followed by his wife Kokopelli-Mana, embellishes a Hohokam bowl from Snaketown, Arizona. Drawing by Heather Hamilton after Gladwin.

to others, such is Kokopelli, the famous hunchbacked flute player, the Kilroy of the Hohokam, thousands of years old but figuratively speaking very much in the present.

Present-day potters, weavers and painters often use the figure as a decoration, perhaps in many instances with no knowledge of the history or the significance of the representation. Fortunately, Kokopelli has never been a sinister character, never voodooistic, but frequently comic.

Kokopelli appears from the San Juan Basin and Monument Valley to Casas Grandes in Mexico, among the Navajos, the Hopis, the Rio Grande pueblos, and others westward to desert California. Not surprisingly, his phallic figure is among the thousands at Arizona's Painted Rocks State Park on the Gila River west of Gila Bend. Early Spanish explorers made note of the rock carvings and called them *piedras pintadas* or painted rocks, although the pictographs actually are incised or scratched rather than painted. Early explorers, trappers and hunters were not noted for their verbal precision.

"Paintings" on the rocks of Piedras Pintadas in Arizona. Browne, 1869.

Kokopelli's likeness varies almost as much as the legends about him, but by and large he is unmistakable, grotesquely hunchbacked, usually phallic in the extreme, and nearly always playing some sort of flute or flageolet.

While some authorities say the flute is a blow-gun, advocates of the musical instrument theory are in the majority. Man has been tooting through a nose pipe since the late Stone Age, virtually all over the world.

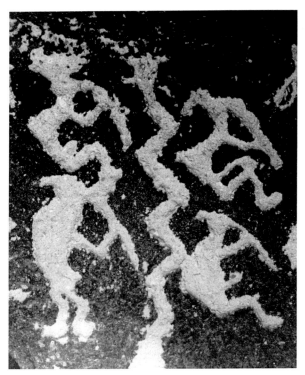

Group of four crude Flute Players and plumed serpent in cave high in a canyon wall in Los Alamos County, New Mexico. The smoke on the white pumice cave wall contrasts with the scratched image. Photograph by John V. Young.

Usually a man's instrument, forbidden to women, was a tube of reed, bone or wood similar to the mouth flute and was played by blowing nostril breath through one end.

Natives of Tahiti used to close one nostril with the thumb while wagging the other fingers along note holes in the tube. Some clans preferred the left nostril, others the right. Some anthropologists surmise that nose music arose from the belief of primitive man that the soul or life-spirit entered and left the body through the nose. The exclamation "God bless you!" — uttered when a person sneezes — may be rooted in the same belief that nostril breath possesses magical powers.

The Kokopelli figure has been found in ruins of pithouse people dating as early as 2OO A.D., and as late as the 16th century where it appears in association with drawings of men on horseback, men armored, and men in cowls.

A modern day rendering of the Flute Player by Gail Haley in **Kokopelli: Drum in Belly,** *2003.*

Arrival of the Spanish conquistadors and missionaries did more than establish an historical date as a base. Through the Inquisition, slavery, starvation, and disease, the natives were all but obliterated. Life in the Southwest was never again the same for Kokopelli and his people.

Before the arrival of the Spaniards, however, pinning down historical dates becomes difficult to the point of impossibility. Something can be learned from the chemistry of the petroglyphs etched on the smooth faces of basaltic cliffs and caves. The drawings are pecked or scratched through the dark brown patina known as desert varnish, the product of centuries of slow oxidation of the minerals in the rock. The artwork exposes lighter-colored rock beneath the patina. Then, over the centuries, the lighter-colored rock will darken again, and in time becomes virtually invisible.

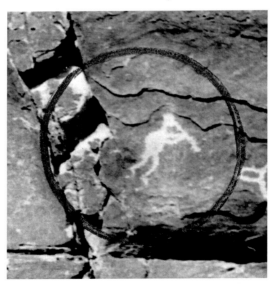

Small figure of Kokopelli at San Cristobal ruin in Mexico. Photograph by John V. Young.

Casual scratchings by vandals are readily apparent because of their color and may be erased by park staff, as they have the ones at Utah's Newspaper Rock State Historic Monument. Displaying thousands of figures, the rocks obviously served as a kind of bulletin board for people with no written alphabet.

Petroglyph display at Newspaper Rock State Historic Monument, located twenty-four miles northwest of Monticello, Utah. Photograph by John V. Young.

Seated, turtle-like figure is a possible variation of Kokopelli often found on Hopi pottery. This group is near San Cristobal ruins southeast of Santa Fe in the Gallisteo Basin. Photograph by John V. Young.

Two of the figures appear to be much older than the others, since they have become much darker than their neighbors. Also, the carvings must have been made when the flood plain at the base of the rock was much higher than it is now. Erosion of the terrain over the centuries has left the top of the rock high and dry, and quite inaccessible without tall ladders.

Another notable feature of the Newspaper Rock carvings is the presence of large, six-toed feet suggesting that there may have been a clan or family of six-toed people who were regarded as gods, or in any case worthy of being reported on the rock. The scientific term for six-toes is polydactylic, which does not help much since it simply means many digits.

Recumbent figure in Tse-Begay Monument Valley. Drawing by Heather Hamilton after photograph by Gilbert Campbell.

Now back to Kokopelli, whose outstanding feature was not his feet.

The reason Kokopelli has a name is fairly simple. The Hopi people of central Arizona, aptly called "archeology on the hoof," make a variety of kachina dolls to sell to tourists. Among the dolls is one they call Kokopelli, and hls "wife" is called Kokopelli-Mana. Kokopelli is hunchbacked and plays a flute.

Formerly, he was vividly phallic, but the missionaries persuaded the Indians to omit this feature in the interests of what they (the missionaries) called decency. The Hopis did not consider sex to be indecent — merely absurd.

Kokopelli-Mana following Kokopelli. Drawing by Heather Hamilton after Gladwin.

Petroglyph of Kokopelli and Shield, or possibly the Sun, at Volcano Cliffs near Albuquerque. Drawing by Heather Hamilton after photograph by Gilbert Campbell.

Like most genuine Kachinas, Kokopelli used to have a human counterpart in a Kachina dancer, the personification of a giant who lived in the mountains. What Kokopelli used to do with explicit gestures to the missionary ladies and female tourists before they learned what the gestures meant, and why the Indians were convulsed with mirth, would be worth elucidating.

Kokopelli's exaggerated phallic appearance could have been due to priapism* or to tuberculosis, or more likely to the common superstition that holds all hunchbacks to be fertility symbols. Many primitive peoples welcomed Kokopelli around corn planting time. Barren wives sought his company; unmarried maidens fled from him in terror.

* Priapus, in both Greek and Roman ancient religious lore, was a fertility god of gardens and herds, the son of Aphrodite and Dionysus. He was depicted as a grotesque little man with an enormous phallus, obviously important in fertility rites.

Two small dancing figures are probably versions of Kokopelli without the flute. These are among many petroglyphs in the San Cristobal ruins. Photograph by John V. Young.

Oraibi women and maidens preparing food. Powell, 1875.

The name Kokopelli may derive from Zuni and Hopi names for a god (Koko), and a desert robber fly they call *pelli*. That predatory insect has a hump on his back and some deplorable habits such as stealing the larvae of other flies. The flute could be the insect's prominent proboscis. Some of the drawings on pottery of the Hohokam and Mimbres people of prehistoric southern Arizona look more like the insect than the man.

Gail E. Haley offers a Jungian take on the Kokopelli story in *Kokopelli: Drum in Belly*. She started thinking about Kokopelli when she noticed that the markings on a cicada shell formed the shape of the hunchbacked Flute Player. Haley suggests that a storyteller or priest among the Anasazi may have seen the same markings and used them as inspiration for a story of how the People came to receive the gifts of fertility and song.

Drawing by Gail E. Haley from Kokopelli: Drum in Belly *(Filter Press, 2003).*

However, it is among the present-day Pueblo people of New Mexico and Arizona that the bulk of the Kokopelli legends were still current until fairly recent times. At San Ildefonso, he was known as a wandering minstrel with a sack of songs on his back. In the Aladdin tradition, he traded new songs for old, and was greeted as a harbinger of fertility and a god of the harvest.

Angular version of Kokopelli in cave on the Pajarito Plateau. Note how the long horn suggests an insect. Photograph by John V. Young.

At Hano, on the Hopi First Mesa, occupied by Pueblo refugees from central New Mexico, Kokopelli and his wife are painted black. He is said to be a character they called Neopkwai'i, which means "big black man." This could be none other than Esteban, the giant Moor who guided Fray Marcos de Niza and his party on their ill-fated exploration of southern Arizona in 1539. Esteban was more interested in the comely Zuni women than he was in the fabled Seven Cities of Cibola, which the party was seeking. When he made passes at the girls, the men decided he was no god after all and shot him full of arrows. Then they buried him under a pile of rocks.

Watching from a safe distance, Marcos de Niza and the rest of the party hastily erected a cross and then took off for Mexico City where they had some hairy tales to tell.

A doorway and ruined wall at Hano, Hopi First Mesa. Mindeleef, 1891.

A terrace view of Zuni Pueblo. Cushing 1883.

At Oraibi, another Hopi village, Kokopelli is said to have a sack of deerskin shirts and moccasins to barter for brides, a modified version of the Esteban legend.

Elsewhere among the Hopis he is said to spend his time sewing on shirts and seducing the daughters of the household while his wife, Kokopelli-Mana, runs after the men.

Kokopelli figures prominently in the obscure Blue Feather legend of the Navajos. This ancient tale says that a wandering Zuni named Blue Feather who was very skillful with throwing sticks (used like dice), bankrupted the great city of Pueblo Bonito in Chaco Canyon (now a national historic park). This action led to the city's downfall in the 13th Century, the story goes. Not satisfied with winning all the tribal treasure and lands, Blue Feather took over the running of the city. His delusions of grandeur led him to woo and win one of the city's sacred vestal virgins. This act of sacrilege brought down the terrible wrath of the gods in the form of drought and disease. The surviving people all ran away and the city collapsed, leaving Blue Feather buried in the ruins.

As man-servant to Blue Feather and bodyguard for the heroine of the piece, the hunchback Kokopelli either died in the ruins with his master, or ran off with the girl according to which version you prefer.

Ruins in Canyon de Chelly. Bickford, 1890.

The Navajo tribe owns and guards one of the finest arrays of Kokopelli figures ever discovered. A long frieze of hunchbacked flute players adorns a large boulder sheltering a small ruin in a remote part of Monument Valley. The ruin was named Flute Player House by the archaeologists who excavated it in 1920.

The real origin of these symbols, like other relics of the arcane Indian world, may be futile to seek in 20th century, Anglo-Saxon terms and modes of thought.

Perhaps there really was a hunchbacked minstrel with an eye for the girls somewhere in the dim past whose memory has come down through the ages like that of the Wandering Jew. Or perhaps the same legend sprang up simultaneously among disparate people with no contact, although this seems unlikely. In any case, the notion of a footloose and hunchbacked flute player with the gift of fertility must have satisfied some deep yearning of the ancient people or they would not have nurtured the legend all the way down to the present day.

White House Ruin in Canyon de Chelly. Bickford, 1890.

Bibliography

Anasazi, Ancient People of the Rock. Photos by David Muench, text by Donald G. Pike. Palo Alto: American West Publishing Co., 1974.

Bickford, F. T. *Prehistoric Cave Dwellings.* Century v. 4 0 (ns 18): 896-911, 1890.

Browne, J. Ross. Adventures in the Apache Country. *Harper's Monthly*, 30, Oct 1864-Mar 1865. Also reprinted U. of Arizona Press, 1974.

Cushing, Frank H. My *Adventures in Zuni.* Century, vols: 25 (1883), 26 (1884). Also Filter Press, 1998.

Cushing, Frank H. *Zuni Fetishes.* Las Vegas: KC Publications, 1966.

At Volcano Cliffs, Albuquerque, Kokopelli with horns resembles Navajo Hunchback God. Drawing by Heather Hamilton after photograph by Gilbert Campbell.

High walls and ladder, Hano, First Mesa Hopi village.
Powell 1875.

Gladwin, Harold S. *A History of the Ancient Southwest.* Portland: Bond Wheelwright, 1957.

Grant, Campbell. *Rock Art of the American Indian.* NY: Crowell, 1967.

Hawley, F. "Kokopelli of the Southwestern Indian Pantheon", *American Anthropologist.* 39: 644-46, 1937.

Mead, George. *Rock Art North of the Mexican Border.* Greeley: Museum of Anthropology. Occasional publications in Anthropology Archeological Series No. 5, 1968.

Mindeleff, Victor A. *A Study of Pueblo Architecture, Tusavan and Cibola.* Washington: Bureau of Ethnology 8th Annual Rept., 1891.

Packard, Gar. *Suns and Serpents.* Santa Fe: Packard Pubs., 1974.

In the Galisteo Basin Kokopelli seems to be wearing a helmet and blowing a horn rather than a flute. A shield or sun symbol is in front of him. Drawing by Heather Hamilton after Muench.

Mummy Cave and Ruin at Canyon del Muerto. Bickford, 1890.

Parsons, E. C. "The Humpbacked Flute Player of the Southwest", *American Anthropologist:* 40:337-388, 1938.

Powell, John Wesley. "Ancient Province of Tusayan", *Scribners Monthly:* 193-213, Dec. 1875.

Renaud, E.B. "Kokopelli: A Study in Pueblo Mythology", *Southwestern Lore,* 14:25-40, 1948.

Schaafsma, Polly. *Early Navaho Rock Painting and Carvings.* Santa Fe Museum of Navaho Ceremonial Art, 1966.

Schaafsma, Polly. *Southwest Indian Pictographs and Petroglyphs.* Santa Fe Museum of New Mexico Press, 1965.

A potbellied Kokopelli toots another horn, St Johns, Arizona. Drawing by Heather Hamilton after Waters.

Tanner, Clara Lee. *Prehistoric Southwestern Craft Arts*. Tucson: University of Arizona Press, 1976.

Thayer, William M. *Marvels of the New West*. Norwich, Conn: Bill Publishing Co., 1892.

Titiev, M. "Story of Kokopelli", *American Anthropologist* 41: 91-98, 1939.

Waters, Frank, and Oswald White Bear Fredericks. *Book of the Hopi*. NY: Viking, 1963.

Wellmann, Klaus F. "Kokopelli of Indian Paleology", *Journal of the American*

Medical Association 212:1678-1682, June 8, 1970

Young, John V. "Peregrinations of Kokopelli", *Westways* (L.A.) 57 no 9: 39-41, Sept. 1965.

Almost identical recumbent figures in Sonora, Mexico (above) and in Canyon de Chelly, Arizona, suggest a Kokopelli resting at home. The Mexican figure, found in a cave, is almost ten feet long. Drawing by Heather Hamilton after Waters.

This horned Kokopelli from Cieneguita, New Mexico, may be the Navajo Hunchback god, who carries a spear or wand and a pack of seeds on his back. He is also called Water Sprinkler. Drawing by Heather Hamilton after Renaud.

More Southwest History and Culture from Filter Press

Kokopelli: Drum in Belly
by Gail E. Haley
Beautifully illustrated and meticulously researched re-interpretation of the Kokopelli story for children.
ISBN: 978-0-86541-069-5. $12.95

Field Mouse Goes to War
by Edward Kennard
Traditional Hopi story for children, bilingual in English and phonetic Hopi. Illustrated by Hopi artist Fred Kabotie.
ISBN: 978-0-86541-046-6. $8.95

Tobacco, Peacepipe, and Indians
by Louis Seig
Examination of the many uses of tobacco among native peoples of North America.
ISBN: 978-0-86541-047-3. $ 4.95

My Adventures in Zuni
Frank H. Cushing's first-person account of his life as the first Anglo to live among the Zuni. First published in 1883-1884.
ISBN: 978-0-86541-045-9. $8.95

The Papago (Tohono O'odham) and Pima Indians of Arizona
Anthropologist Ruth M. Underhill describes everyday life, religion, arts, and government of two Arizona tribes.
ISBN: 978-0-86541-059-6 $10.95.

Pueblo Crafts
Anthropologist Ruth M. Underhill's survey of crafts among the Pueblo cultures.
ISBN: 978-0-910584-51-7. $12.00

Southwestern Indian Recipe Book
by Zora Hesse
A collection of traditional aboriginal recipes with a few modern variations.
ISBN: 978-0-86541-042-8 $ 4.95

These and other titles are available by calling 888-570-2663 and on-line at FilterPressBooks.com.